# Songs of the Fields by Francis Ledwidge

Francis Ledwidge was born in Slane, Ireland on 19th August 1887 to a poor family, the eighth of nine children whose father died when he was 5 years old.

Despite the family's encouragement for education these circumstances meant Francis was forced to leave his local school at 13 and seek whatever work he could.  He had a range of jobs including as a copper miner which resulted in him becoming a trade union activist and secretary to his local branch of the Meath Labour Union in 1913.  Self educated and always in his spare time writing poems which were published in local journals, Francis attracted a well known man of letters and patronage who was well connected in literary circles both in Dublin and London - Lord Dunsany.   This brought his work to the attention of among others WB Yeats and Katherine Tynan and resulted in the publication of his first, and well received, collection of poetry entitled Songs of the Fields.

However, Francis was an active patriot and nationalist who due to Ireland's involvement in the WWI enlisted, despite the offer of a regular stipend from Dunsany if he did not go to war and a faction of Irish nationalists condemning fighting with the British.

His army career serving with the 1st Battalion of the Irish Regiment the Royal Inniskilling Fusiliers was successful with him rapidly becoming a lance corporal.

Ledwidge fought at Gallipoli and continued throughout the war years to write poems.

On July 31st 1917 whilst road laying for the Battle of Ypres a German artillery shell exploded and it was reported 'Ledwidge killed. blown to bits'.  He was 29 years old.

There is a memorial near Ypres dedicated to his memory and he is buried nearby at Artillery Wood cemetery.

The cottage where he was born is now a museum as his work has subsequently been celebrated by an ever increasing public and formed part of the Irish school syllabus where he is known as the Poet of the Blackbird.

## Index of Contents

INTRODUCTION by LORD DUNSANY

If one who looked from a tower for a new star, watching for years
the same part of the sky, suddenly saw it (quite by chance while

thinking of other things), and knew it for the star for which he had hoped, how many millions of men would never care?

And the star might blaze over deserts and forests and seas, cheering lost wanderers in desolate lands, or guiding dangerous quests; millions would never know it.

And a poet is no more than a star. If one has arisen where I have so long looked for one, amongst the Irish peasants, it can be little more than a secret that I shall share with those who read this book because they care for poetry.

I have looked for a poet amongst the Irish peasants because it seemed to me that almost only amongst them there was in daily use a diction worthy of poetry, as well as an imagination capable of dealing with the great and simple things that are a poet's wares. Their thoughts are in the spring-time, and all their metaphors fresh: in London no one makes metaphors any more, but daily speech is strewn thickly with dead ones that their users should write upon paper and give to their gardeners to burn.

In this same London, two years ago, where I was wasting June, I received a letter one day from Mr. Ledwidge and a very old copy-book. The letter asked whether there was any good in the verses that filled the copy-book, the produce apparently of four or five years. It began with a play in verse that no manager would dream of, there were mistakes in grammar, in spelling of course, and worse—there were such phrases as "'thwart the rolling foam," "waiting for my true love on the lea," etc., which are vulgarly considered to be the appurtenances of poetry; but out of these and many similar errors there arose continually, like a mountain sheer out of marshes, that easy fluency of shapely lines which is now so noticeable in all that he writes; that and sudden glimpses of the fields that he seems at times to bring so near to one that one exclaims,

"Why, that is how Meath looks," or "It is just like that along the Boyne in April," quite taken by surprise by familiar things: for none of us knows, till the poets point them out, how many beautiful things are close about us.

Of pure poetry there are two kinds, that which mirrors the beauty of the world in which our bodies are, and that which builds the more mysterious kingdoms where geography ends and fairyland begins, with gods and heroes at war, and the sirens singing still, and Alph going down to the darkness from Xanadu. Mr. Ledwidge gives us the first kind. When they have read through the profounder poets, and seen the problem plays, and studied all the perplexities that puzzle man in the cities, the small circle of readers that I predict for him will turn to Ledwidge as to a mirror reflecting beautiful fields, as to a very still lake rather on a very cloudless evening.

There is scarcely a smile of Spring or a sigh of Autumn that is not reflected here, scarcely a phase of the large benedictions of Summer; even of Winter he gives us clear glimpses sometimes, albeit mournfully, remembering Spring.

"In the red west the twisted moon is low,
And on the bubbles there are half-lit stars:
Music and twilight: and the deep blue flow
Of water: and the watching fire of Mars.
The deep fish slipping through the moonlit bars
Make death a thing of sweet dreams,—"

What a Summer's evening is here.

And this is a Summer's night in a much longer poem that I have not included in this selection, a summer's night seen by two lovers:

"The large moon rose up queenly as a flower
Charmed by some Indian pipes. A hare went by,

A snipe above them circled in the sky."

And elsewhere he writes, giving us the mood and picture of Autumn in a single line:

"And somewhere all the wandering birds have flown."

With such simple scenes as this the book is full, giving nothing at all to those that look for a " message," but bringing a feeling of quiet from gleaming Irish evenings, a book to read between the Strand and Piccadilly Circus amidst the thunder and hootings.

To every poet is given the revelation of some living thing so intimate that he speaks, when he speaks of it, as an ambassador speaking for his sovereign; with Homer it was the heroes, with Ledwidge it is the small birds that sing, but in particular especially the blackbird, whose cause he champions against all other birds almost with a vehemence such as that with which men discuss whether Mr.— , M.P., or his friend the Right Honourable — is really the greater ruffian. This is how he speaks of the blackbird in one of his earliest poems; he was sixteen when he wrote it, in a grocer's shop in Dublin, dreaming of Slane, where he was born; and his dreams turned out to be too strong for the grocery business, for he walked home one night, a distance of thirty miles :

"Above me smokes the little town
With its whitewashed walls and roofs of brown
And its octagon spire toned smoothly down
As the holy minds within.
And wondrous, impudently sweet,
Half of him passion, half conceit,
The blackbird calls adown the street,
Like the piper of Hamelin."

Let us not call him the Burns of Ireland, you who may like this book, nor even the Irish John Clare, though he is more like him, for poets

6

are all incomparable (it is only the versifiers that resemble the great ones) but let us know him by his own individual song: he is the poet of the blackbird.

I hope that not too many will be attracted to this book on account of the author being a peasant, lest he come to be praised by the how-interesting! school; for know that neither in any class, nor in any country, nor in any age, shall you predict the footfall of Pegasus, who touches the earth where he pleaseth and is bridled by whom he will.

**DUNSANY.**
*June, 1914.*

I wrote this preface in such a different June, that if I sent it out with no addition it would make the book appear to have dropped a long while since out of another world, a world that none of us remembers now, in which there used to be leisure.

Ledwidge came last October into the 5th Battalion of the Royal Inniskilling Fusiliers, which is in one of the divisions of Kitchener's first army, and soon earned a lance-corporal's stripe.

All his future books lie on the knees of the gods. May They not be the only readers. Any well-informed spy can probably tell you our movements, so of such things I say nothing.

**DUNSANY, Captain,**
*June, 1915. 5th R. Inniskilling Fusiliers.*

TO MY BEST FRIEND

I love the wet-lipped wind that stirs the hedge

And kisses the bent flowers that drooped for rain,
That stirs the poppy on the sun-burned ledge
And like a swan dies singing, without pain.
The golden bees go buzzing down to stain
The lilies' frills, and the blue harebell rings,
And the sweet blackbird in the rainbow sings.

Deep in the meadows I would sing a song,
The shallow brook my tuning-fork, the birds
My masters; and the boughs they hop along
Shall mark my time: but there shall be no words
For lurking Echo's mock; an angel herds
Words that I may not know, within, for you,
Words for the faithful meet, the good and true.


## BEHIND THE CLOSED EYE

I walk the old frequented ways
That wind around the tangled braes,
I live again the sunny days
Ere I the city knew.

And scenes of old again are born,
The woodbine lassoing the thorn,
And drooping Ruth-like in the corn
The poppies weep the dew.

Above me in their hundred schools
The magpies bend their young to rules,
And like an apron full of jewels
The dewy cobweb swings.

And frisking in the stream below
The troutlets make the circles flow,

And the hungry crane doth watch them grow
As a smoker does his rings.

Above me smokes the little town,
With its whitewashed walls and roofs of brown
And its octagon spire toned smoothly down
As the holy minds within.

And wondrous impudently sweet,
Half of him passion, half conceit,
The blackbird calls adown the street
Like the piper of Hamelin.

I hear him, and I feel the lure
Drawing me back to the homely moor,
I'll go and close the mountains' door
On the city's strife and din.


## BOUND TO THE MAST

When mildly falls the deluge of the grass,
And meads begin to rise like Noah's flood,
And o'er the hedgerows flow, and onward pass,
Dribbling thro' many a wood;
When hawthorn trees their flags of truce unfurl,
And dykes are spitting violets to the breeze;
When meadow larks their jocund flight will curl
From Earth's to Heaven's leas;

Ah! then the poet's dreams are most sublime,
A-sail on seas that know a heavenly calm,
And in his song you hear the river's rhyme,
And the first bleat of the lamb.
Then when the summer evenings fall serene,

9

Unto the country dance his songs repair,
And you may meet some maids with angel mien,
Bright eyes and twilight hair.

When Autumn's crayon tones the green leaves sere,
And breezes honed on icebergs hurry past;
When meadow-tides have ebbed and woods grow drear,
And bow before the blast;
When briars make semicircles on the way;
When blackbirds hide their flutes and cower and die;
When swollen rivers lose themselves and stray
Beneath a murky sky;

Then doth the poet's voice like cuckoo's break,
And round his verse the hungry lapwing grieves,
And melancholy in his dreary wake
The funeral of the leaves.
Then when the Autumn dies upon the plain,
Wound in the snow alike his right and wrong,
The poet sings, albeit a sad strain,
Bound to the Mast of Song.


TO A LINNET IN A CAGE

When Spring is in the fields that stained your wing,
And the blue distance is alive with song,
And finny quiets of the gabbling spring
Rock lilies red and long,
At dewy daybreak, I will set you free
In ferny turnings of the woodbine lane,
Where faint-voiced echoes leave and cross in glee
The hilly swollen plain.

In draughty houses you forget your tune,

The modulator of the changing hours,
You want the wide air of the moody noon,
And the slanting evening showers.
So I will loose you, and your song shall fall
When morn is white upon the dewy pane,
Across my eyelids, and my soul recall
From worlds of sleeping pain.


## A TWILIGHT IN MIDDLE MARCH

Within the oak a throb of pigeon wings
Fell silent, and grey twilight hushed the fold,
And spiders' hammocks swung on half-oped things
That shook like foreigners upon our cold.
A gipsy lit a fire and made a sound
Of moving tins, and from an oblong moon
The river seemed to gush across the ground
To the cracked metre of a marching tune.

And then three syllables of melody
Dropped from a blackbird's flute, and died apart
Far in the dewy dark. No more but three,
Yet sweeter music never touched a heart
Neath the blue domes of London. Flute and reed,
Suggesting feelings of the solitude
When will was all the Delphi I would heed,
Lost like a wind within a summer wood
From little knowledge where great sorrows brood.


## SPRING

The dews drip roses on the meadows

11

Where the meek daisies dot the sward.
And Æolus whispers through the shadows,
"Behold the handmaid of the Lord!"
The golden news the skylark waketh
And 'thwart the heavens his flight is curled
Attend ye as the first note breaketh
And chrism droppeth on the world.

The velvet dusk still haunts the stream
Where Pan makes music light and gay.
The mountain mist hath caught a beam
And slowly weeps itself away.
The young leaf bursts its chrysalis
And gem-like hangs upon the bough,
Where the mad throstle sings in bliss
O'er earth's rejuvenated brow.

**ENVOI**

Slowly fall, O golden sands,
Slowly fall and let me sing,
Wrapt in the ecstasy of youth,
The wild delights of Spring.

DESIRE IN SPRING

I love the cradle songs the mothers sing
In lonely places when the twilight drops,
The slow endearing melodies that bring
Sleep to the weeping lids; and, when she stops,
I love the roadside birds upon the tops
Of dusty hedges in a world of Spring.

And when the sunny rain drips from the edge
Of midday wind, and meadows lean one way,
And a long whisper passes thro' the sedge,
Beside the broken water let me stay,
While these old airs upon my memory play,
And silent changes colour up the hedge.


## A RAINY DAY IN APRIL

When the clouds shake their hyssops, and the rain
Like holy water falls upon the plain,
'Tis sweet to gaze upon the springing grain
And see your harvest born.

And sweet the little breeze of melody,
The blackbird puffs upon the budding tree,
While the wild poppy lights upon the lea
And blazes 'mid the corn.

The skylark soars the freshening shower to hail,
And the meek daisy holds aloft her pail,
And Spring all radiant by the wayside pale,
Sets up her rock and reel.

See how she weaves her mantle fold on fold,
Hemming the woods and carpeting the wold.
Her warp is of the green, her woof the gold,
The spinning world her wheel.

By'n by above the hills a pilgrim moon
Will rise to light upon the midnight noon,
But still she plieth to the lonesome tune
Of the brown meadow rail.

No heavy dreams upon her eyelids weigh,
Nor do her busy fingers ever stay;
She knows a fairy prince is on the way
To wake a sleeping beauty.

To deck the pathway that his feet must tread,
To fringe the 'broidery of the roses' bed,
To show the Summer she but sleeps, not dead,
This is her fixed duty.


## ENVOI

To-day while leaving my dear home behind,
My eyes with salty homesick teardrops blind,
The rain fell on me sorrowful and kind
Like angels' tears of pity.

'Twas then I heard the small birds' melodies,
And saw the poppies' bonfire on the leas,
As Spring came whispering thro' the leafing trees
Giving to me my ditty.


## A SONG OF APRIL

The censer of the eglantine was moved
By little lane winds, and the watching faces
Of garden flowerets, which of old she loved,
Peep shyly outward from their silent places.
But when the sun arose the flowers grew bolder,
And she will be in white, I thought, and she
Will have a cuckoo on her either shoulder,
And woodbine twines and fragrant wings of pea.

And I will meet her on the hills of South,
And I will lead her to a northern water,
My wild one, the sweet beautiful uncouth,
The eldest maiden of the Winter's daughter.
And down the rainbows of her noon shall slide
Lark music, and the little sunbeam people,
And nomad wings shall fill the river side,
And ground winds rocking in the lily's steeple.


## THE BROKEN TRYST

The dropping words of larks, the sweetest tongue
That sings between the dusks, tell all of you;
The bursting white of Peace is all along
Wing-ways, and pearly droppings of the dew
Emberyl the cobwebs' greyness, and the blue
Of hiding violets, watching for your face,
Listen for you in every dusky place.

You will not answer when I call your name,
But in the fog of blossom do you hide
To change my doubts into a red-faced shame
By'n by when you are laughing by my side?
Or will you never come, or have you died,
And I in anguish have forgotten all?
And shall the world now end and the heavens fall?


## THOUGHTS AT THE TRYSTING STILE

Come, May, and hang a white flag on each thorn,
Make truce with earth and heaven; the April child
Now hides her sulky face deep in the morn

Of your new flowers by the water wild
And in the ripples of the rising grass,
And rushes bent to let the south wind pass
On with her tumult of swift nomad wings,
And broken domes of downy dandelion.
Only in spasms now the blackbird sings.
The hour is all a-dream.

Nets of woodbine
Throw woven shadows over dreaming flowers,
And dreaming, a bee-luring lily bends
Its tender bell where blue dyke-water cowers
Thro' briars, and folded ferns, and gripping ends
Of wild convolvulus.

          The lark's sky-way
Is desolate.
        I watch an apple-spray
Beckon across a wall as if it knew
I wait the calling of the orchard maid.
Inly I feel that she will come in blue,
With yellow on her hair, and two curls strayed
Out of her comb's loose stocks, and I shall steal

Behind and lay my hands upon her eyes,
"Look not, but be my Psyche!"
                And her peal
Of laughter will ring far, and as she tries
For freedom I will call her names of flowers
That climb up walls ; then thro' the twilight hours
We'll talk about the loves of ancient queens,
And kisses like wasp-honey, false and sweet,
And how we are entangled in love's snares
Like wind-looped flowers.

## EVENING IN MAY

There is nought tragic here, tho' night uplifts
A narrow curtain where the footlights burned,

But one long act where Love each bold heart sifts
And blushes in the dark, but has not spurned

The strong resolve of noon. The maiden's head
Is brown upon the shoulder of her youth,

Hearts are exchanged, long pent up words are said,
Blushes burn out at the long tale of truth.

The blackbird blows his yellow flute so strong,
And rolls away the notes in careless glee,

It breaks the rhythm of the thrushes' song,
And puts red shame upon his rivalry.

The yellowhammers on the roof tiles beat
Sweet little dulcimers to broken time,

And here the robin with a heart replete
Has all in one short plagiarised rhyme.

## AN ATTEMPT AT A CITY SUNSET

(TO J. K. Q.)

There was a quiet glory in the sky
When thro' the gables sank the large red sun,
And toppling mounts of rugged cloud went by

Heavy with whiteness, and the moon had won
Her way above the woods, with her small star
Behind her like the cuckoo's little mother. . . .
It was the hour when visions from some far
Strange Eastern dreams like twilight bats take wing
Out of the ruin of memories.

                    O brother
Of high song, wand'ring where the Muses fling
Rich gifts as prodigal as winter rain,
Like stepping-stones within a swollen river
The hidden words are sounding in my brain,
Too wild for taming; and I must for ever
Think of the hills upon the wilderness,
And leave the city sunset to your song.
For there I am a stranger like the trees
That sigh upon the traffic all day long.


## WAITING

A strange old woman on the wayside sate,
Looked far away and shook her head and sighed.
And when anon, close by, a rusty gate
Loud on the warm winds cried,
She lifted up her eyes and said, "You're late."
Then shook her head and sighed.

And evening found her thus, and night in state
Walked thro' the starlight, and a heavy tide
Followed the yellow moon around her wait,
And morning walked in wide.
She lifted up her eyes and said, "You're late."
Then shook her head and sighed.

## THE SINGER'S MUSE

I brought in these to make her kitchen sweet,
Haw blossoms and the roses of the lane.
Her heart seemed in her eyes so wild they beat
With welcome for the boughs of Spring again.
She never heard of Babylon or Troy,
She read no book, but once saw Dublin town;
Yet she made a poet of her servant boy
And from Parnassus earned the laurel crown.

If Fame, the Gorgon, turns me into stone
Upon some city square, let someone place
Thorn blossoms and lane roses newly blown
Beside my feet, and underneath them trace:
"His heart was like a bookful of girls' song,
With little loves and mighty Care's alloy.
These did he bring his muse, and suffered long,
Her bashful singer and her servant boy."


## INAMORATA

The bees were holding levees in the flowers,
Do you remember how each puff of wind
Made every wing a hum? My hand in yours
Was listening to your heart, but now
The glory is all faded, and I find
No more the olden mystery of the hours
When you were lovely and our hearts would bow
Each to the will of each, but one bright day.
Is stretching like an isthmus in a bay
From the glad years that I have left behind.

I look across the edge of things that were
And you are lovely in the April ways,
Holy and mute, the sigh of my despair. . . .
I hear once more the linnets' April tune
Beyond the rainbow's warp, as in the days
You brought me facefuls of your smiles to share
Some of your new-found wonders. ... Oh when soon
I'm wandering the wide seas for other lands,
Sometimes remember me with folded hands,
And keep me happy in your pious prayer.


## THE WIFE OF LLEW

And Gwydion said to Math, when it was Spring:
"Come now and let us make a wife for Llew."
And so they broke broad boughs yet moist with dew,
And in a shadow made a magic ring:
They took the violet and the meadow-sweet
To form her pretty face, and for her feet
They built a mound of daisies on a wing
And for her voice they made a linnet sing
In the wide poppy blowing for her mouth.
And over all they chanted twenty hours.
And Llew came singing from the azure south
And bore away his wife of birds and flowers.


## THE HILLS

The hills are crying from the fields to me,
And calling me with music from a choir
Of waters in their woods where I can see

The bloom unfolded on the whins like fire.
And, as the evening moon climbs ever higher
And blots away the shadows from the slope,
They cry to me like things devoid of hope.

Pigeons are home. Day droops. The fields are cold.
Now a slow wind comes labouring up the sky
With a small cloud long steeped in sunset gold,
Like Jason with the precious fleece anigh
The harbour of Iolcos. Day's bright eye
Is filmed with the twilight, and the rill
Shines like a scimitar upon the hill.

And moonbeams drooping thro' the coloured wood
Are full of little people winged white.
I'll wander thro' the moon-pale solitude
That calls across the intervening night
With river voices at their utmost height,
Sweet as rain-water in the blackbird's flute
That strikes the world in admiration mute.


JUNE

Broom out the floor now, lay the fender by,
And plant this bee-sucked bough of woodbine there,
And let the window down. The butterfly
Floats in upon the sunbeam, and the fair
Tanned face of June, the nomad gipsy, laughs
Above her widespread wares, the while she tells
The farmers' fortunes in the fields, and quaffs
The water from the spider-peopled wells.

The hedges are all drowned in green grass seas,
And bobbing poppies flare like Elmor's light,

While siren-like the pollen-stained bees
Drone in the clover depths. And up the height
The cuckoo's voice is hoarse and broke with joy.
And on the lowland crops the crows make raid,
Nor fear the clappers of the farmer's boy,
Who sleeps, like drunken Noah, in the shade.

And loop this red rose in that hazel ring
That snares your little ear, for June is short
And we must joy in it and dance and sing,
And from her bounty draw her rosy worth.
Ay! soon the swallows will be flying south,
The wind wheel north to gather in the snow,
Even the roses spilt on youth's red mouth
Will soon blow down the road all roses go.


IN MANCHESTER

There is a noise of feet that move in sin
Under the side-faced moon here where I stray,
Want by me like a Nemesis. The din
Of noon is in my ears, but far away
My thoughts are, where Peace shuts the blackbirds' wings
And it is cherry time by all the springs.

And this same moon floats like a trail of fire
Down the long Boyne, and darts white arrows thro'
The mill wood; her white skirt is on the weir,
She walks thro' crystal mazes of the dew,
And rests awhile upon the dewy slope
Where I will hope again the old, old hope.

With wandering we are worn my muse and I,
And, if I sing, my song knows nought of mirth.

I often think my soul is an old lie
In sackcloth, it repents so much of birth.
But I will build it yet a cloister home
Near the peace of lakes when I have ceased to roam.


## MUSIC ON WATER

Where does Remembrance weep when we forget?
From whither brings she back an old delight?
Why do we weep that once we laughed? and yet
Why are we sad that once our hearts were light?
I sometimes think the days that we made bright
Are damned within us, and we hear them yell,
Deep in the solitude of that wide hell,
Because we welcome in some new regret.

I will remember with sad heart next year
This music and this water, but to-day
Let me be part of all this joy. My ear
Caught far-off music which I bid away,
The light of one fair face that fain would stay
Upon the heart's broad canvas, as the Face
On Mary's towel, lighting up the place.
Too sad for joy, too happy for a tear.

Methinks I see the music like a light
Low on the bobbing water, and the fields
Yellow and brown alternate on the height,
Hanging in silence there like battered shields,
Lean forward heavy with their coloured yields
As if they paid it homage; and the strains,
Prisoners of Echo, up the sunburnt plains
Fade on the cross-cut to a future night.

In the red West the twisted moon is low,
And on the bubbles there are half-lit stars:
Music and twilight: and the deep blue flow
Of water: and the watching fire of Mars:
The deep fish slipping thro' the moonlit bars
Make Death a thing of sweet dreams, life a mock.
And the soul patient by the heart's loud clock
Watches the time, and thinks it wondrous slow.


TO M. McG.

(WHO CAME ONE DAY WHEN WE WERE ALL GLOOMY AND
CHEERED US WITH SAD MUSIC)

We were all sad and could not weep,
Because our sorrow had not tears:
You came a silent thing like Sleep,
And stole away our fears.

Old memories knocking at each heart
Troubled us with the world's great lie:
You sat a little way apart
And made a fiddle cry.

And April with her sunny showers
Came laughing up the fields again:
White wings went flashing thro' the hours
So lately full of pain.

And rivers full of little lights
Came down the fields of waving green:
Our immemorial delights
Stole in on us unseen.

For this may Good Luck let you loose
Upon her treasures many years,
And Peace unfurl her flag of truce
To any threat'ning fears.


## IN THE DUSK

Day hangs its light between two dusks, my heart,
Always beyond the dark there is the blue.
Sometime we'll leave the dark; myself and you,
And revel in the light for evermore.
But the deep pain of you is aching smart,
And a long calling weighs upon you sore.

Day hangs its light between two dusks, and song
Is there at the beginning and the end.
You, in the singing dusk, how could you wend
The songless way Contentment fleetly wings?
But in the dark your beauty shall be strong,
Tho' only one should listen how it sings.


## THE DEATH OF AILILL

When there was heard no more the war's loud sound,
And only the rough corn-crake filled the hours,
And hill winds in the furze and drowsy flowers,
Maeve in her chamber with her white head bowed
On Ailill's heart was sobbing: "I have found
The way to love you now," she said, and he
Winked an old tear away and said: "The proud
Unyielding heart loves never." And then she:
"I love you now, tho' once when we were young

We walked apart like two who were estranged
Because I loved you not, now all is changed."
And he who loved her always called her name
And said: "You do not love me, 'tis your tongue
Talks in the dusk; you love the blazing gold
Won in the battles, and the soldier's fame.
You love the stories that are often told
By poets in the hall." Then Maeve arose
And sought her daughter Findebar: "O, child,
Go tell your father that my love went wild
With all my wars in youth, and say that now
I love him stronger than I hate my foes. ..."
And Findebar unto her father sped
And touched him gently on the rugged brow,
And knew by the cold touch that he was dead.


## AUGUST

She'll come at dusky first of day,
White over yellow harvest's song.
Upon her dewy rainbow way
She shall be beautiful and strong.
The lidless eye of noon shall spray
Tan on her ankles in the hay,
Shall kiss her brown the whole day long.

I'll know her in the windrows, tall
Above the crickets of the hay.
I'll know her when her odd eyes fall,
One May-blue, one November-grey.
I'll watch her from the red barn wall
Take down her rusty scythe, and call,
And I will follow her away.

THE VISITATION OF PEACE

I closed the book of verse where Sorrow wept
Above Love's broken fane where Hope once prayed,
And thought of old trysts broken and trysts kept
Only to chide my fondness. Then I strayed
Down a green coil of lanes where murmuring wings
Moved up and down like lights upon the sea,
Searching for calm amid untroubled things
Of wood and water. The industrious bee
Sang in his barn within the hollow beech,
And in a distant haggard a loud mill
Hummed like a war of hives. A whispered speech
Of corn and wind was on the yellow hill,
And tattered scarecrows nodded their assent
And waved their arms like orators. The brown
Nude beauty of the Autumn sweetly bent
Over the woods, across the little town.

I sat in a retreating shade beside
The river, where it fell across a weir
Like a white mane, and in a flourish wide
Roars by an island field and thro' a tier
Of leaning sallies, like an avenue
When the moon's flambeau hunts the shadows out
And strikes the borders white across the dew.
Where little ringlets ended, the fleet trout

Fed on the water moths. A marsh hen crossed
On flying wings and swimming feet to where
Her mate was in the rushes forest, tossed
On the heaving dusk like swallows in the air.

Beyond the river a walled rood of graves

Hung dead with all its hemlock wan and sere,
Save where the wall was broken and long waves
Of yellow grass flowed outward like a weir,
As if the dead were striving for more room
And their old places in the scheme of things;
For sometimes the thought comes that the brown tomb
Is not the end of all our labourings,
But we are born once more of wind and rain,
To sow the world with harvest young and strong,
That men may live by men 'til the stars wane,
And still sweet music fill the blackbird's song.

But O for truths about the soul denied.
Shall I meet Keats in some wild isle of balm,
Dreaming beside a tarn where green and wide
Boughs of sweet cinnamon protect the calm
Of the dark water ? And together walk
Thro' hills with dimples full of water where
White angels rest, and all the dead years talk
About the changes of the earth ? Despair
Sometimes takes hold of me but yet I hope
To hope the old hope in the better times
When I am free to cast aside the rope
That binds me to all sadness 'till my rhymes
Cry like lost birds. But O, if I should die
Ere this millennium, and my hands be crossed
Under the flowers I loved, the passers-by
Shall scowl at me as one whose soul is lost.

But a soft peace came to me when the West
Shut its red door and a thin streak of moon
Was twisted on the twilight's dusky breast.
It wrapped me up as sometimes a sweet tune
Heard for the first time wraps the scenes around,
That we may have their memories when some hand
Strikes it in other times and hopes unbound

Rising see clear the everlasting land.


## BEFORE THE TEARS

You looked as sad as an eclipsed moon
Above the sheaves of harvest, and there lay
A light lisp on your tongue, and very soon
The petals of your deep blush fell away;
White smiles that come with an uneasy grace
From inner sorrow crossed your forehead fair,
When the wind passing took your scattered hair
And flung it like a brown shower in my face.

Tear-fringed winds that fill the heart's low sighs
And never break upon the bosom's pain,
But blow unto the windows of the eyes
Their misty promises of silver rain,
Around your loud heart ever rose and fell.
I thought 'twere better that the tears should come
And strike your every feeling wholly numb,
So thrust my hand in yours and shook farewell.


## GOD'S REMEMBRANCE

There came a whisper from the night to me
Like music of the sea, a mighty breath
From out the valley's dewy mouth, and Death
Shook his lean bones, and every coloured tree
Wept in the fog of morning. From the town
Of nests among the branches one old crow
With gaps upon his wings flew far away.
And, thinking of the golden summer glow,

I heard a blackbird whistle half his lay
Among the spinning leaves that slanted down.

And I who am a thought of God's now long
Forgotten in His Mind, and desolate
With other dreams long over, as a gate
Singing upon the wind the anvil song,
Sang of the Spring when first He dreamt of me
In that old town all hills and signs that creak:—
And He remembered me as something far
In old imaginations, something weak
With distance, like a little sparking star
Drowned in the lavender of evening sea.


## AN OLD PAIN

What old, old pain is this that bleeds anew?
What old and wandering dream forgotten long
Hobbles back to my mind? With faces two,
Like Janus of old Rome, I look about,
And yet discover not what ancient wrong
Lies unrequited still. No speck of doubt
Upon to-morrow's promise. Yet a pain
Of some dumb thing is on me, and I feel
How men go mad, how faculties do reel
When these old querns turn round within the brain.

'Tis something to have known one day of joy,
Now to remember when the heart is low,
An antidote of thought that will destroy
The asp bite of Regret. Deep will I drink
By'n by the purple cups that overflow,
And fill the shattered heart's urn to the brink.
But some are dead who laughed! Some scattered are

Around the sultry breadth of foreign zones.
You, with the warm clay wrapt about your bones,
Are nearer to me than the live afar.

My heart has grown as dry as an old crust,
Deep in book lumber and moth-eaten wood,
So long it has forgot the old love lust,
So long forgot the thing that made youth dear,
Two blue love lamps, a heart exceeding good,
And how, when first I heard that voice ring clear
Among the sering hedges of the plain,
I knew not which from which beyond the corn,
The laughter by the callow twisted thorn,
The jay-thrush whistling in the haws for rain.

I hold the mind is the imprisoned soul,
And all our aspirations are its own
Struggles and strivings for a golden goal,
That wear us out like snow men at the thaw.
And we shall make our Heaven where we have sown
Our purple longings. Oh! can the loved dead draw
Anear us when we moan, or watching wait
Our coming in the woods where first we met,
The dead leaves falling on their wild hair wet,
Their hands upon the fastenings of the gate?

This is the old, old pain come home once more,
Bent down with answers wild and very lame
For all my delving in old dog-eared lore
That drove the Sages mad. And boots the world
Aught for their wisdom? I have asked them, tame,
And watched the Earth by its own self be hurled
Atom by atom into nothingness,
Loll out of the deep canyons, drops of fire,
And kindle on the hills its funeral pyre,
And all we learn but shows we know the less.

## THE LOST ONES

Somewhere is music from the linnets' bills,
And thro' the sunny flowers the bee-wings drone,
And white bells of convolvulus on hills
Of quiet May make silent ringing, blown
Hither and thither by the wind of showers,
And somewhere all the wandering birds have flown;
And the brown breath of Autumn chills the flowers.

But where are all the loves of long ago?
Oh, little twilight ship blown up the tide,
Where are the faces laughing in the glow
Of morning years, the lost ones scattered wide?
Give me your hand, Oh brother, let us go
Crying about the dark for those who died.

## ALL-HALLOWS EVE

Thedreadful hour is sighing for a moon
To light old lovers to the place of tryst,
And old footsteps from blessed acres soon
On old known pathways will be lightly prest;
And winds that went to eavesdrop since the noon,

Kinking* at some old tale told sweetly brief,
Will give a cowslick** to the yarrow leaf,***
And sling the round nut from the hazel down.

*Provincially a kind of laughter.*

32

**A curl of hair thrown back from the forehead: used metaphorically here, and itself a metaphor taken from the curl of a cow's tongue.

***Maidens on Hallows Eve pull leaves of yarrow, and, saying over them certain words, put them under their pillows and so dream of their true-loves.*

And there will be old yarn balls,* and old spells
In broken lime-kilns, and old eyes will peer
For constant lovers in old spidery wells,**
And old embraces will grow newly dear.
And some may meet old lovers in old dells,
And some in doors ajar in towns light-lorn;—
But two will meet beneath a gnarly thorn
Deep in the bosom of the windy fells.
Then when the night slopes home and white-faced day
Yawns in the east there will be sad farewells;
And many feet will tap a lonely way
Back to the comfort of their chilly cells,
And eyes will backward turn and long to stay
Where love first found them in the clover bloom
But one will never seek the lonely tomb,
And two will linger at the tryst alway.

*They also throw balls of yarn (which must be black) over their left shoulders into old lime-kilns, holding one end and then winding it in till they feel it somehow caught, and expect to see in the darkness the face of their lover.

**Also they look for his face in old wells.*

A MEMORY

Low sounds of night that drip upon the ear,
The plumed lapwing's cry, the curlew's call,
Clear in the far dark heard, a sound as drear
As raindrops pelted from a nodding rush
To give a white wink once and broken fall
Into a deep dark pool: they pain the hush,
As if the fiery meteor's slanting lance
Had found their empty craws: they fill with sound
The silence, with the merry round,
The sounding mazes of a last year's dance.

I thought to watch the stars come spark by spark
Out on the muffled night, and watch the moon
Go round the full, and turn upon the dark,
And sharpen towards the new, and waiting watch
The grand Kaleidoscope of midnight noon
Change colours on the dew, where high hills notch
The low and moony sky. But who dare cast
One brief hour's horoscope, whose tuned ear
Makes every sound the music of last year?
Whose hopes are built up in the door of Past?

No, not more silent does the spider stitch
A cobweb on the fern, nor fogdrops fall
On sheaves of harvest when the night is rich
With moonbeams, than the spirits of delight
Walk the dark passages of Memory's hall.
We feel them not, but in the wastes of night
We hear their low-voiced mediums, and we rise
To wrestle old Regrets, to see old faces,
To meet and part in old tryst-trodden places
With breaking heart, and emptying of eyes.

I feel the warm hand on my shoulder light,
I hear the music of a voice that words
The slow time of the feet, I see the white

Arms slanting, and the dimples fold and fill....
I hear wing-flutters of the early birds,
I see the tide of morning landward spill,
The cloaking maidens, hear the voice that tells
"You'd never know" and "Soon perhaps again,"
With white teeth biting down the inly pain,
Then sounds of going away and sad farewells.

A year ago! It seems but yesterday.
Yesterday! And a hundred years! All one.
Tis laid a something finished, dark, away,
To gather mould upon the shelves of Time.
What matters hours or aeons when 'tis gone?
And yet the heart will dust it of its grime,
And hover round it in a silver spell,
Be lost in it and cry aloud in fear;
And like a lost soul in a pious ear,
Hammer in mine a never easy bell.


A SONG


My heart has flown on wings to you, away
In the lonely places where your footsteps lie
Full up of stars when the short showers of day
Have passed like ancient sorrows. I would fly
To your green solitude of woods to hear
You singing in the sounds of leaves and birds;
But I am sad below the depth of words
That nevermore we two shall draw anear.

Had I but wealth of land and bleating flocks
And barnfuls of the yellow harvest yield,
And a large house with climbing hollyhocks
And servant maidens singing in the field,

You'd love me; but I own no roaming herds,
My only wealth is songs of love for you,
And now that you are lost I may pursue
A sad life deep below the depth of words.


## A FEER

I roamed the woods to-day and seemed to hear,
As Dante heard, the voice of suffering trees.
The twisted roots seemed bare contorted knees,
The bark was full of faces strange with fear.

I hurried home still wrapt in that dark spell,
And all the night upon the world's great lie
I pondered, and a voice seemed whisp'ring nigh,
"You died long since, and all this thing is hell!"


## THE COMING POET

"Is it far to the town?" said the poet,
As he stood 'neath the groaning vane,
And the warm lights shimmered silver
On the skirts of the windy rain.
"There are those who call me," he pleaded,
"And I'm wet and travel sore."
But nobody spoke from the shelter,
And he turned from the bolted door.

And they wait in the town for the poet
With stones at the gates, and jeers,
But away on the wolds of distance
In the blue of a thousand years

He sleeps with the age that knows him,
In the clay of the unborn, dead,
Rest at his weary insteps,
Fame at his crumbled head.


## THE VISION ON THE BRINK

To-night when you sit in the deep hours alone,
And from the sleeps you snatch wake quick and feel
You hear my step upon the threshold-stone,
My hand upon the doorway latchward steal,
Be sure 'tis but the white winds of the snow,
For I shall come no more.

And when the candle in the pane is wore,
And moonbeams down the hill long shadows throw,
When night's white eyes are in the chinky door,
Think of a long road in a valley low,
Think of a wanderer in the distance far,
Lost like a voice among the scattered hills.

And when the moon has gone and ocean spills
Its waters backward from the trysting bar,
And in dark furrows of the night there tills
A jewelled plough, and many a falling star
Moves you to prayer, then will you think of me
On the long road that will not ever end.

Jonah is hoarse in Nineveh I'd lend
My voice to save the town and hurriedly
Goes Abraham with murdering knife, and Ruth
Is weary in the corn. . . . Yet will I stay,
For one flower blooms upon the rocks of truth,
God is in all our hurry and delay.

## TO LORD DUNSANY

### (ON HIS RETURN FROM EAST AFRICA)

For you I knit these lines, and on their ends
Hang little tossing bells to ring you home.
The music is all cracked, and Poesy tends
To richer blooms than mine; but you who roam
Thro' coloured gardens of the highest muse,
And leave the door ajar sometimes that we
May steal small breathing things of reds and blues
And things of white sucked empty by the bee,
Will listen to this bunch of bells from me.

My cowslips ring you welcome to the land
Your muse brings honour to in many a tongue,
Not only that I long to clasp your hand,
But that you're missed by poets who have sung
And viewed with doubt the music of their verse
All the long winter, for you love to bring
The true note in and say the wise thing terse,
And show what birds go lame upon a wing,
And where the weeds among the flowers do spring.


## ON AN OATEN STRAW

MY harp is out of tune, and so I take
An oaten straw some shepherd dropped of old.
It is the hour when Beauty doth awake
With trembling limbs upon the dewy cold.
And shapes of green show where the woolly fold

38

Slept in the winding shelter of the brake.

This I will pipe for you, how all the year
The one I love like Beauty takes her way.
Wrapped in the wind of winter she doth cheer
The loud woods like a sunbeam of the May.
This I will pipe for you the whole blue day
Seated with Pan upon the mossy weir.


## EVENING IN FEBRUARY

The windy evening drops a grey
Old eyelid down across the sun,
The last crow leaves the ploughman's way,
And happy lambs make no more fun.

Wild parsley buds beside my feet,
A doubtful thrush makes hurried tune,
The steeple in the village street
Doth seem to pierce the twilight moon.

I hear and see those changing charms,
For all my thoughts are fixed upon
The hurry and the loud alarms
Before the fall of Babylon.


## THE SISTER

I saw the little quiet town,
And the whitewashed gables on the hill,
And laughing children coming down
The laneway to the mill.

Wind-blushes up their faces glowed,
And they were happy as could be,
The wobbling water never flowed
So merry and so free.

One little maid withdrew aside
To pick a pebble from the sands.
Her golden hair was long and wide,
And there were dimples on her hands.

And when I saw her large blue eyes,
What was the pain that went thro' me?
Why did I think on Southern skies
And ships upon the sea?


BEFORE THE WAR OF COOLEY

At daybreak Maeve rose up from where she prayed
And took her prophetess across her door
To gaze upon her hosts. Tall spear and blade
Burnished for early battle dimly shook
The morning's colours, and then Maeve said:
                              "Look
And tell me how you see them now."
                              And then
The woman that was lean with knowledge said:
"There's crimson on them, and there's dripping red."
And a tall soldier galloped up the glen
With foam upon his boot, and halted there
Beside old Maeve. She said, "Not yet," and turned
Into her blazing dun, and knelt in prayer
One solemn hour, and once again she came
And sought her prophetess. With voice that mourned,

40

"How do you see them now?" she asked.
                                  "All lame
And broken in the noon." And once again
The soldier stood before her.
                                  "No, not yet."
Maeve answered his inquiring look and turned
Once more unto her prayer, and yet once more
"How do you see them now?" she asked.
                                  "All wet
With storm rains, and all broken, and all tore
With midnight wolves." And when the soldier came
Maeve said, "It is the hour." There was a flash
Of trumpets in the dim, a silver flame
Of rising shields, loud words passed down the ranks,
And twenty feet they saw the lances leap.
They passed the dun with one short noisy dash.
And turning proud Maeve gave the wise one thanks,
And sought her chamber in the dun to weep.


## LOW-MOON LAND

I often look when the moon is low
Thro' that other window on the wall,
At a land all beautiful under snow,
Blotted with shadows that come and go
When the winds rise up and fall.
And the form of a beautiful maid
In the white silence stands,
And beckons me with her hands.

And when the cares of the day are laid,
Like sacred things, in the mart away,
I dream of the low-moon land and the maid
Who will not weary of waiting, or jade

Of calling to me for aye.
And I would go if I knew the sea
That lips the shore where the moon is low,
For a longing is on me that will not go.


## THE SORROW OF FINDEBAR

"Why do you sorrow, child? There is loud cheer
In the wide halls, and poets red with wine
Tell of your eyebrows and your tresses long,
And pause to let your royal mother hear
The brown bull low amid her silken kine.
And you who are the harpstring and the song
Weep like a memory born of some old pain."

And Findebar made answer, "I have slain
More than Cuculain's sword, for I have been
The promised meed of every warrior brave
In Tain Bo Cualigne wars, and I am sad
As is the red banshee that goes to keen
Above the wet dark of the deep brown grave,
For the warm loves that made my memory glad."

And her old nurse bent down and took a wild
Curl from her eye and hung it on her ear,
And said, "The woman at the heavy quern,
Who weeps that she will never bring a child,
And sees her sadness in the coming year,
Will roll up all her beauty like a fern;
Not you, whose years stretch purple to the end."

And Findebar, "Beside the broad blue bend
Of the slow river where the dark banks slope
Wide to the woods sleeps Ferdia apart.

I loved him, and then drove him for pride's sake
To early death, and now I have no hope,
For mine is Maeve's proud heart, Ailill's kind heart,
And that is why it pines and will not break."


## ON DREAM WATER

And so, o'er many a league of sea
We sang of those we left behind.
Our ship split thro' the phosphor free,
Her white sails pregnant with the wind,
And I was wondering in my mind
How many would remember me.

Then red-edged dawn expanded wide,
A stony foreland stretched away,
And bowed capes gathering round the tide
Kept many a little homely bay.
O joy of living there for aye,
O Soul so often tried!


## THE DEATH OF SUALTEM

After the brown bull passed from Cooley's fields
And all Muirevne was a wail of pain,
Sualtem came at evening thro' the slain
And heard a noise like water rushing loud,
A thunder like the noise of mighty shields.
And in his dread he shouted: "Earth is bowed,
The heavens are split and stars make war with stars
And the sea runs in fear!"
                        For all his scars

He hastened to Dun Dealgan, and there found
It was his son, Cuculain, making moan.
His hair was red with blood, and he was wound
In wicker full of grass, and a cold stone
Was on his head.

                 "Cuculain, is it so?"
Sualtem said, and then, "My hair is snow,
My strength leaks thro' my wounds, but I will die
Avenging you."

               And then Cuculain said:
"Not so, old father, but take horse and ride
To Emain Macha, and tell Connor this."
Sualtem from his red lips took a kiss,
And turned the stone upon Cuculain's head.
The Lia-Macha with a heavy sigh
Ran up and halted by his wounded side.
In Emain Macha to low lights and song
Connor was dreaming of the beauteous Maeve.
He saw her as at first, by Shannon's wave,
Her insteps in the water, mounds of white.
It was in Spring, and music loud and strong
Rocked all the coloured woods, and the blue height
Of heaven was round the lark, and in his heart
There was a pain of love.

             Then with a start
He wakened as a loud voice from below
Shouted, " The land is robbed, the women shamed,
The children stolen, and Cuculain low!"
Then Connor rose, his war-worn soul inflamed,
And shouted down for Cathbad; then to greet
The messenger he hurried to the street.
And there he saw Sualtem shouting still
The message of Muirevne 'mid the sound
Of hurried bucklings and uneasy horse.
At sight of him the Lia-Macha wheeled,
So that Sualtem fell upon his shield,

And his grey head came shouting to the ground.
They buried him by moonlight on the hill,
And all about him waves the heavy gorse.


## THE MAID IN LOW-MOON LAND

I know not where she be, and yet
I see her waiting white and tall.
Her eyes are blue, her lips are wet,
And move as tho' they'd love to call.
I see her shadow on the wall
Before the changing moon has set.

She stands there lovely and alone
And up her porch blue creepers swing.
The world she moves in is her own,
To sun and shade and hasty wing.
And I would wed her in the Spring,
But only I sit here and moan.


## THE DEATH OF LEAG, CUCHULAIN'S CHARIOTEER

**CONALL**
"I only heard the loud ebb on the sand,
The high ducks talking in the chilly sky.
The voices that you fancied floated by
Were wind notes, or the whisper on the trees.
But you are still so full of war's red din,
You hear impatient hoof-beats up the land
When the sea's changing, or a lisping breeze
Is playing on the waters of the linn."

**LEAG**

"I hear Cuchulain's voice, and Emer's voice,
The Lia Macha's neigh, the chariot's wheels,
Farther away a bell bough's drowsy peals;
And sleep lays heavy thumbs upon my eyes.
I hear Cuchulain sing above the chime
Of One Who comes to make the world rejoice,
And comes again to blot away the skies,
To wipe away the world and roll up Time."

**CONALL**

"In the dark ground forever mouth to mouth
They kiss thro' all the changes of the world,
The grey sea fogs above them are unfurled
At evening when the sea walks with the moon,
And peace is with them in the long cairn shut.
You loved him as the swallow loves the South,
And Love speaks with you since the evening put
Mist and white dews upon short shadowed noon."

**LEAG**

"Sleep lays his heavy thumbs upon my eyes,
Shuts out all sounds and shakes me at the wrists.
By Nanny water where the salty mists
Weep o'er Riangabra let me stand deep
Beside my father. Sleep lays heavy thumbs
Upon my eyebrows, and I hear the sighs
Of far loud waters, and a troop that comes
With boughs of bells—"

**CONALL**

"They come to you with sleep."


THE PASSING OF CAOILTE

'Twas just before the truce sang thro' the din
Caoilte, the thin man, at the war's red end
Leaned from the crooked ranks and saw his friend
Fall in the farther fury; so when truce
Halted advancing spears the thin man came
And bending by pale Oscar called his name;
And then he knew of all who followed Finn'
He only felt the cool of Gavra's dews.

And Caoilte, the thin man, went down the field
To where slow water moved among the whins,
And sat above a pool of twinkling fins
To court old memories of the Fenian men,
Of how Finn's laugh at Conan's tale of glee
Brought down the rowan's boughs on Knocnaree,
And how he made swift comets with his shield
At moonlight in the Fomar's rivered glen.

And Caoilte, the thin man, was weary now,
And nodding in short sleeps of half a dream:
There came a golden barge down middle stream,
And a tall maiden coloured like a bird
Pulled noiseless oars, but not a word she said.
And Caoilte, the thin man, raised up his head
And took her kiss upon his throbbing brow,
And where they went away what man has heard?


GROWING OLD

We'll fill a Provence bowl and pledge us deep
The memory of the far ones, and between
The soothing pipes, in heavy-lidded sleep,
Perhaps we'll dream the things that once have been.

Tis only noon and still too soon to die,
Yet we are growing old, my heart and I.

A hundred books are ready in my head
To open out where Beauty bent a leaf.
What do we want with Beauty? We are wed
Like ancient Proserpine to dismal grief.
And we are changing with the hours that fly,
And growing odd and old, my heart and I.

Across a bed of bells the river flows,
And roses dawn, but not for us; we want
The new thing ever as the old thing grows
Spectral and weary on the hills we haunt.
And that is why we feast, and that is why
We're growing odd and old, my heart and I.


## AFTER MY LAST SONG

Where I shall rest when my last song is over
The air is smelling like a feast of wine;
And purple breakers of the windy clover
Shall roll to cool this burning brow of mine;
And there shall come to me, when day is told,
The peace of sleep when I am grey and old.

I'm wild for wandering to the far-off places
Since one forsook me whom I held most dear.
I want to see new wonders and new faces
Beyond East seas; but I will win back here
When my last song is sung, and veins are cold
As thawing snow, and I am grey and old.

Oh paining eyes, but not with salty weeping,

My heart is like a sod in winter rain;
Ere you will see those baying waters leaping
Like hungry hounds once more, how many a pain
Shall heal; but when my last short song is trolled
You'll sleep here on wan cheeks grown thin and old.


## FRANCIS LEDWIDGE – A CONCISE BIBLIOGRAPHY

Songs of the Fields (1915)
Songs of Peace (1917)
Last Songs (1918)
The complete poems of Francis Ledwidge; with introductions by
Lord Dunsany (1919)

www.ingramcontent.com/pod-product-compliance
Lightning Source LLC
Chambersburg PA
CBHW021944040426
42448CB00008B/1234